OIL PASTEL ESSENTIALS

The Ultimate Guide for Beginners

Abigail Brian

Table of Contents

CHAPTER ONE

INTRODUCTION

Would you say you are attracted to the malleable nature and sparkling completion of oil paints? Do you like taking on new difficulties with antiquated, wonderful, silly designs? Is the way that you ought to paint vast vehicles conveying you a sketchy skilled worked with fit? If you're looking for a depiction of yourself, you've come to the ideal districts since oil pastels give you more than you typically suspect. To figure out more, infer this oil pastel bearing book, made expressly for vivacious adults.

Why Oil Pastels?

Youngsters will appreciate utilizing the mix of shade, oil, and wax. Sakura in 1925 devised oil pastels and called it Insane Pas. Correspondingly that oil paint works in an essential game plan, the rich outline solid areas for makes. Follow a general youth's manual for oil pastels and transport your inside ace with get-together and innovative cerebrum. The versatile rich course of action gives help out you to quickly start making workmanship by dislodging paintbrushes, extensions, and solvents. In this way, oil does not contaminate or incapacitate materials that have been worked with. People of all ages kids, showed informed specialists, students, and, immensely, even the old can without an absolutely radiant stretch apply these silly pastels. With the appropriate shocking tones, base your innovative cerebrum on your substance and grant the scene to stimulate interest. Anyway, before entering the pastel world, we ought to take a gander at the stray pieces. Is it conceivable that pastels ought to draw a great deal of additional idea from you? Perceive How to consolidate oil pastels for beginners before long.

What precisely are oil glues?

The astonishing creation sticks are made of ground tone and a folio made of oil or wax that doesn't dry out. Experts can blend and preparation in with a grouping of impact roads considering the way that the drawing medium has a rich and smooth surface. The smooth surface of the stick awards you to draw anything you need on it paper, board, material, wood, glass, a wall, or even a stone. Oil pastels are easy to utilize, testing to utilize, and require unessential idea. You simply need the dependable pastels, some paper, and an old surface that you can administer without pounding to learn pastels.

Do you additionally truly prefer to paint with watercolors?

See the watercolor supplies: goofs to stay away from while utilizing watercolors to paint. Because of their moderate nature, pastels are notable among understudies.

The medium is not difficult to pass, and giving various outcomes and approaches can be used. Oil pastels can be utilized either totally dry or blended, mixed, scratched off, made to show up, obviously, to be wet paint, given an oil finish, or blended and mixed. The medium is ideal for imaginative and interested non-affected individuals.

Have you truly purchased additional pastels yet are dangerous where to begin?

Take a gander at The Focal of Oil Pastels How to Use oil pastel and get everything moving! The minor obedient goliath central development will have you completely twirling around the rich mixes! In such manner, get your pastels and get blending. There are different get-togethers of oil pastels, each with its own characteristics and applications. Before purchasing the most stunning shades, determine what suits your requirements the best. There are essentially five sorts of pastels.

Touchy Pastels

The most notable pastels have broadcasting energies yet get little thought. This is the best framework for picking one. Taking into account its rich surface and fragile consistency, it is obviously certified for layering and blending to make dazzling painterly outcomes. Because of its tricky course of action and smooth surface, Delicate

Pastels is viewed as reasonable for experts in the business. These pastels are used to make general arrangements in different shapes, including square, change, thick, pitiful, and long-to-short.

Hard Pastels

Hard pastels are reliable for precise or point-by-point work like drawing and painting because they have more folio and fewer shades. It works astoundingly together and adds vast last nuances. When used with fragile pastels it produces changed astounding craftsmanship. Hard pastels have their sharp, dull lines when the shade, water, and cover are great. Skillet Pastels Dish pastels are a stunning sort of pastel that are held inside compartments or holders, as the name proposes. It is additionally protected, simple to store, and underscores the fundamental pastel blend in the game plan. They can be involved on various surfaces and genuinely capacity as one. Utilization of paintbrushes and other connection upset is a certain need in holder pastels.

PENCIL PASTELS AND HOLDER PASTELS

We know a ton about hard and delicate pastels, yet we really want to understand what the plan is for the center. Pencil pastels are the ideal mix and consistency of fragile and hard pastels encased in a pencil case. The plan grants specialists bound, point-by-point access. Pencil pastels were worked with unequivocally for you expecting that you're looking for the astonishing experience of pastels while comparably wanting to avoid the disaster area! General's Pastel Pencil, Stabilo CarbOthello Pastel Pencil, Faber-Castell Pitt Pastel Pencils, Derwent Pastel Pencils, and Koh-I-Noor Gioconda Pastel Pencils are among the striking brands of pencil pastels.

QUALITY FOR UNDERSTUDIES AND SPECIALISTS

There are two boss grades of oil pastels that are open for acquiring: Nature of the Expert and Nature of the

Understudy extraordinarily far between the two is the level of shade to get. In the expert's quality, there is a further level of shade to the catch and subsequently, the mix is more grounded and really limit. Specialists should simply use this, and it costs stunningly more too. The stick is more excited and has an effect on the quality of the understudy, but it uses more catch or filler. It's fitting that youngsters need to find out about the astounding universe of plan and craftsmanship.

The upkeep and fundamental relationship of the expert's not forever gotten up in a position blend, which a basic pastel piece. Layering, a huge oil pastel technique, is very important, and the tones in the virtuoso quality reflect this flawlessness. Colors are constantly blended while layering with the hair-raising pastels of the students. In any case, the student quality set's sensibility and adaptability demonstrate that it is appropriate for students. Because of the separation in quality among expert and understudy oil pastels, teenagers ought to buy sets as opposed to individual pastels. Regardless of how this is reasonable, it gets clients far from picking unequivocal mixes. There is an assortment of oil pastel set covers.

CHAPTER TWO

SURFACE FOR OIL PASTELS

Oil pastels can be used on different surfaces in view of their adaptability. There is a great deal of data accessible in regards to the probability of the oil pastels' mind boggling perfection, no matter what the mode where we should be. Since oil pastels never totally dry, it's conceivable that they will spread and give our astounding show-stopper the presence of being a tangled wreck. Oil pastels can be utilized on rocks, paper, cardboard, materials, wood, and glass, clearly! Papers with a ton of tooth are beneficial over those with a smoother surface concerning the oil pastels' outer layer.

Surface for Oil Pastels as a great deal of spilling out over getting ready and cleaning should be possible with horrendous quality papers. In any case, working with oil pastels on heavyweight paper is an incredible choice. To ensure that your work of art doesn't cross hurt by not having an ideal surface, you can do whatever it takes not to use oil pastels with a smooth idea. Before you pick a surface for your creation, you ought to close what kind of painting you really need to make. Might you need to provide your craftsmanship with the energy of turpentine? Do you vivaciously benefit by the chance to paint with oil pastels in a more standard manner? Everything is depicted by your reaction. While planning to manage a drawing, pastel paper is an ideal choice. In any case, it doesn't go with the mineral effect. While picking mineral spirits for your masterpiece, watercolor paper and material paper are your go-to resources. Gather your supplies, including pastels of your choice, a clear sheet, and your own workspace! With this enormous oil pastel sidekick, you can get ready to make your most important gemstone. Keep in mind that as you learn new techniques and skills, you get closer to your goal. While working with oil pastels, the most huge and undeniable methodology is to blend! While working with oil pastels, the specialty of mixing is immense. Mix in with your fingers, a piece of paper towel, or even a material.

Blending

Regardless, pick a pastel of your choice and rub it on a piece of paper. Rub it cautiously to make a cloudy or shadowy appearance. Center around the stream or advancement of the blend. The more you blend the more the assortment will change. Thusly, you can join various shades. Have different contacts with this strategy.

Customs of Mixing Oil Pastels:

1. Applying the tones uninhibitedly may not yield the best shades of oil pastels;

2. Blending quickly with one's fingers; applying the pastels with clear tension is best since utilizing battling strain could leave white in the center. It will not just make your fingers shake, yet it will similarly feature your strength in a jumbled manner.

Do's of Blending Oil Pastels

1. Use solid strain and don't leave white paper under.

2. To ensure a uniform blend, use superfluous meandering enhancements where the shades of blends are covering; To ensure a smooth new development, move past the various hues of groupings. Do you truly have to be aware of the most

well-known technique for mixing? Despite the fact that blending can be fulfilling here and there, it can likewise be savage and perilous on the off chance that the right contemplations aren't utilized. Subsequently, we prescribe perusing.

How to Set with Oil Pastels:

Methodologies for blending oil pastels that look astounding together. Cushioning structures a zenith like stroke, as its name proposes. Make a tuft like line that will add surface to your claim to fame. Do you review when we made stunning strokes with makes arrangements for our disturbing journals as children? Like padding, draw short vertical strokes on the paper. Plan to orchestrate this arrangement. Start making feather strokes by picking two or three spots that are around two shades of your choice. Totally when you hope to have achieved the most raised degree of layering possible. Apply more strain close to the beginning and let it free towards the upward end. Similar to padding, scumbling is a layering technique for oil pastel designs. Make standard controlled structure shows on a shallow level with a few tones, contingent upon your inclination.

Scumbling

This strategy is convincing and muddling as you should in basically the same manner far as could genuinely be expected! Keep on covering until you accomplish the best surface or appearance. Take the necessary steps not to be aggravated by the lines' straightness, thickness, or division in any capacity you can. You can blend it later. Covering is a way of thinking that includes isolating pastel pearl's edges and lines. Since pastels require sharpness, conveying great and conscious edges with them can challenge. To avoid this issue, veiling and covering are utilized only when absolutely necessary. Cover the spots you would rather not variety in with a pastel of your decision. Use the pastels in the spaces between the tapes. Dispose of the tape when you're finished and feel a responsibility of appreciation in your craftsmanship with unequivocal lines and edges. The most common method for monitoring the development of surface-specked deserts is wrapping. Children can't resist the urge to use this framework and practice to deal with their abilities. End Partake in this game plan and notice the surface's overall perceptible real factors without zeroing in on consistency. You can give your work a lot of surface and perspective by using this procedure from the oil pastel juvenile's manual.

TIPS AND INSIGHTS OF OIL PASTLES

1. Could we at some point be certain?

Making pastels can be a chaotic business. Oil pastels' adaptability can make it trying to give your convincing artistic work described edges. Likewise, on the off chance that you genuinely need to avoid this calamity, you can push toward your magnum opus with sureness. Not solely will giving your indications give them a more certain appearance, but it will comparably enhance your work. Fill your material with colors after you frame it. As youngsters, this methodology generally speaking worked, in your adulthood or learning stage, these undertakings to follow.

2. Do you study the chief piece of workmanship you made?

Was there a wonderful plot? The awesome blossom or your #1 brightened up character? It could very well be the all-encompassing view with the squashed vegetation, the shockingly active sun between two mountains, a small stream, and your small house? We for the most part in obviously had started with head notwithstanding pictures. Furthermore, if you're basically starting, you should start with significant shapes, figures, or still pictures. Before moving on to more obfuscated figures, gradually develop your viewpoints.

Would you like to draw an oil pastel dusk like the one you and I used to draw as children? Take a gander at Oil pastel drawing, Dusk scene every single push toward turn.

Skipping into the enabled and exceptional universe of oil pastels can astonish in any event piece of the time, regardless, overwhelming. You may be appealed to utilize different changed conceals immediately. Fight with the allurement and rudeness mixing such boundless assortments continually out. Like the saying "such a giant number of cooks ruin the stock," utilizing such vast assortments will reduce the meaning of your drawing.

CONCENTRATE ON THE GOOD AND THE BAD, BIT BY BIT

You'll change pastel brands starting with one brand then onto the accompanying. Furthermore, temperature impacts the hardness and non-abrasiveness of the pastels. In warm temperatures, oil pastels are more brittle than in cool ones. Hence, using and assessing different brands to close your sensibility and love is a stunning cycle.

CHAPTER THREE

OIL PASTELS BRAND FOR LEARNERS

The continuous consequence of oil pastels for youths can expect the piece of the legend for a youngster investigating the cloudy waters of strategies.

I. Sommelier Oil Pastels: The sensational high color tones are the most popular choice among experts from all walks of life. They are gushing out, energized, and strong. Accordingly, if you really need a specialist magnum opus, buy your Sommelier Oil Pastels here.

II. Sakura Oil Pastels: The particular and amazing Sakura Insane Pas oil pastels are really easy to blend. The more you push them, the additional amazing they become. Thusly, get these phenomenal smooth shades today and thought them a doorway on watercolor papers, faint shade papers, sandpaper see, streak foam or another surface.

III. Caran d'Ache Neopastels: The novel pastels are resistant to water. Because of its smooth, fragile surface, it is great to work with it. It will be utilized on cowhide, acrylic, stone, wood, glass, and fundamentally all the other things.

IV. Pentel Articulations' Oil Pastels: Pentel Verbalizations Oil pastels are an excellent choice for young people due to their dependable mix. They are comical and easy to utilize, pursuing them an astounding decision for entertainment only, imaginative characters.

V. Crayola Oil Pastels: Layer down your creative brain with the rich, smooth Crayolastels. Whether you really need to go for complete clouding or made drawing, Crayola Oil Pastels are the pick.

VI. Oil Pastels by Prima: For mixing and layering colors, Prima Oil Pastels are ideal by virtue of their extraordinary perfection. Layer and blend a lot of these rich tones to make your little masterpiece thusly.

VII. Faber-Castel Oil Pastels: Is it veritable that you are looking for pastels that are huge, pretty, and reasonable? The

Faber-Castel Oil pastels are suitable for everyone due to their ease of use and wide range of shades.

VIII. Oil Pastels from Reeves: The mix of 48 obvious choices is ideal for camouflage, drawing, and blueprint, despite various things. Furthermore, the smooth, clear tones are usable on various surfaces. Last tests show that painting is the best place. Find out about the preposterousness and lively blueprint medium to examine the field of craftsmanship. Oil pastels can be utilized as a compensatory medium if appropriately controlled. Our real juvenile's oil pastel guide will give you a solid understanding of the pastel world.

Proceed and throw several stunning tones on a sheet and pour out your innovative cerebrum. Remember, painting is about interest, inventive mind, and the unconstrained improvement of assessments. Generally award your hands to move while your free inventive cerebrum streams. Continue to rehearse and don't surrender on the grounds that each gifted laborer was once a fledgling. This is our associate for specialists on the most effective way to draw with oil pastels. The best method for using oil pastels It recalls data for how to mix and what materials to purchase. Oil pastel is quite possibly of the freshest inventive procedure that anybody could expect to find. It was made during the twentieth 100 years, but the case that it was facilitated by Picasso isn't definitively undeniable - it was first developed as a vehicle for youths in Japan. (The Spanish master did, anyway, work with the French producer Sommelier during the 1940s to develop its line of expert grade oil pastels, which are over an extended time used across the world.) Specialists today are having a lot of familiarity with oil pastels by virtue of their fortitude and speed. Several experts use them as the underpinnings of their oil show-stoppers but they can also advance noteworthy drawings through their own endeavor. They're astoundingly versatile, so are electrifying contraptions to assemble in your pack expecting that you like drawing outside.

Regardless, oil pastels can be attempting to work with, especially for individuals who are more used to painting. While there are a ton of crossbreeds between oil paint and oil pastels, they each work to their own guidelines. With pastels, you have a restricted degree of blends to research, so you ought to be express, and to make sense of how pastels can be layered and controlled. We'll walk you through everything you need to get started with this amazing, unrestricted medium, including how to mix and draw, in our guide to drawing with oil pastels. This is followed up by our pick of the best oil pastels to buy. Oil pastel is one of the newest creative techniques available. It was made during the 20th 100 years, at this point the case that it was prepared by Picasso isn't precisely obviously undeniable, it was first developed as a plan for youths in Japan. The Spanish master did, in any case, work with the French maker Sommelier during the 1940s to energize its line of master grade oil pastels, which are at present used across the world. Oil pastels are conspicuous among experts today for the strength and astuteness they offer. They can be used as a foundation for oil compositions by certain professionals, but they can also be used to make beautiful drawings on their own. Since they are so common to use, they are an extraordinary gadget to keep in your backpack if you like to head outside. In any case, working with oil pastels can be testing, especially for experienced craftsmen. While there are a great deal of mutts between oil paint and oil pastels, they each work to their own guidelines. Since there are simply such incalculable likely groupings with pastels, you should be clear about how pastels can be layered and controlled. We'll walk you through everything you need to get started with this amazing, unrestricted medium, including how to mix and draw, in our guide to drawing with oil pastels. We'll examine tricks and strategies for extra cultivated performers as well as how to coordinate oil pastels for young people. To help you in benefitting from your oil pastel craftsmanship, we with having other than investigated a part for the best materials to buy.

How truly oil pastels limit?

Hide sticks are bound together by wax and oil that doesn't dry out, similar to linseed oil, in oil pastels. Oil pastels, in contrast to wax shaded pencils, have a distinct character due to the use of oil: When applied unintentionally, they can be astoundingly flaky; however they can comparatively be controlled and made in various layers of game plan. This is a huge idea since oil pastels could get turbulent. Colors have an inclination for getting across pastels, and, like oil painting, it's basic for them to spread. Commitments to work in used articles of clothing and bring some kitchen towels or paper towels with you.

While making oil pastels, do you combine water?

Oil pastels can be utilized without the utilization of water; however specific kinds of oil pastels should be water-solvent.

Are oil pastels clear for youngsters?

We suggest oil pastels for kids! They're extremely easy to progress at whatever point you've controlled a few direct procedures. It is reachable for any kind of future family, considering everything.

Do you begin with light or dull oil pastels while working with them?

Layering lighter oil pastels over extra faint ones is never-ending. While drawing your subject, consider its light and mid-tones before finally progressing forward toward the haziest darks.

Do you ever consider using an oil pastel brush at some point?

Utilize a brush to streamline your drawing in the event that you are mixing your oil pastels in with mineral oil or even more humble. For this, we recommend custom-made paint brushes or ones designed specifically for oil paints.

CHAPTER FOUR

CONSISTENTLY RULES TO BLEND OIL PASTELS

Oil pastels can be blended easily. Mixing your drawing or partitions of it can have different effects; especially expecting that you do it instead of leaving all-over wrote engraves. Oil pastels can be mixed in various ways. Coming up next are a few strategy to help you with starting:

1. Pastel on pastel. Oil pastels can be layered on top of each other, and scoured together so they blend in assortment. Anyway, this ought to be done with obstacle: Exactly when your surface shows up at a particular point, it basically can't get through assortment.

2. Your fingers. This is the kind of thing you'll need to do cautiously, as you can without a really excellent stretch wipe normal lubes from your fingers into your pastels. A stunning choice would be a blending stump.

3. Froth for pipe security. It's not something you'll get up at your close by craftsmanship store, yet it's a marvelously remarkable thing among oil pastel informed prepared experts: It is truly gifted at solidifying tones as one.

4. Any more thin for oil paint. Utilizing a firm brush and mineral spirits like turpentine, oil paint can be spread into certifiable spreads routinely around the paper. Notwithstanding the way that a dangerous material ought to be moved cautiously, it dries quickly. From mixing stumps to kid oil, there are many systems you can attempt to consolidate your pastels. Take a gander at our how to blend oil pastels guide for extra tips and bewilders.

MAKING IT EVERY LITTLE STEP HEADINGS TO DRAW WITH OIL PASTELS

The best method for concluding a reasonable procedure for drawing with oil pastels is to play out different quick evaluations and investigate various streets concerning stamp creation and different layering frameworks. You'll quickly find how oil pastels act, and what you can achieve with them. Coming up next are a simple methods for involving oil pastels for novices:

1. Back scratch. Graffito, or scratching into your drawing with an appear at edge or the culmination of a paintbrush, is a phenomenal technique for adding purpose in mixing. Yet again colors from prior layers should be apparent.

2. Be careful while picking your blends. You ought to utilize each of the arrangements you have accessible to you without a second thought. The colors orange and blue work well together; red

and green; yellow and purple - can be used together to convey eye-drop by results.

3. Keep your hands clean while you work. Oil pastels are not difficult to clear out from your hands in the event that you utilize a cleaning trained professional and water while you are working. Place a piece of paper under it to draw with your convincing work.

4. Strive to do whatever it takes not to use foul arrangements. The probability of pastels having chaotic, cross-ruined tips increments as you layer them. While you are working, keep one more piece of paper promptly accessible. You can use this to discard the pastels' untidy tips

before applying a new, scattered combination stroke.

5. In chromatic control, large oil pastel techniques should be kept in mind. We can promise you that you will be grateful all through a somewhat long time. At the point when pastels are organized in a blend, it is a lot more straightforward to track down them.

This is only a short design of some restoring oil pastel procedures for juveniles; Look at our oil pastel systems guide for extra contemplations. Oil pastels are beyond question an item where spending somewhat more can have a major effect. These are the best oil pastels to buy. Monetary technique sets of oil pastels are for the most part around colossal on wax and missing the mark on stow away. You'll find them less rich in assortment and less layer able: They don't legitimize the work. Sommelier, the most widely recognized brand for oil pastels, produces a particularly captivating 48-party assortment. Any oil pastel-skilled prepared proficient would adore this arrangement of expert grade pastels.

BEST PAPER FOR OIL PASTELS

Oil pastels can be applied to different grades of paper. We propose you review various surfaces and tones. Oil pastels work best on paper with a feeble or fair tone: you'll find that light assortments stand bound more. Strathmore, one of our most notable paper brands, has different pastel-obliging papers to peruse.

Sprinkle fixative

Spot resources in a compartment piled up with sprinkle fixative. Other immense materials for gifted oil pastel talented specialists It will abstain from spreading or confusing while away. By fixing the drawing's surface, you'll have the option to apply extra tones significantly more rapidly and without any problem.

Mineral spirits

We suggest Punch It, a citrus-based even areas of strength for less soul that is neither burnable nor hazardous and can utilized in mix. It is more secure for use in the home than turpentine or white soul and, for certain, has a really enrapturing fragrance.

Blending stumps

Blending stumps are paper contributes that are a fundamental piece of the energy used to smooth out oil pastel drawings. They are sensible and will chip away at it to draw with clean hands. Right when they get foul, you can clean the tip with a mould able eraser or rub it with sandpaper. At long last, you should be ready to get everything rolling on your own oil pastel creation. Good luck!

Educative action: Painting with oil pastels are a fantastic procedure for pushing conveying energies. For our oil pastel demo under, we worked from a reference photo of a Cotswold's wood in the pre-winter.

You will require:

1. Oil pastels

2. Oil paint diluents

3. Blended media paper

4. Paint brush

STEP BY STEP GUIDE ON PAINTING OIL PASTELS

Stage 1: Making what's going on We began the drawing by drawing free lines and making plans to separate the warm tones of the leaves from the cool shadows on the pathway.

Stage 2: Adding surface to your drawing after the diluting disappeared completely, we added additional surfaces and nuances to the under drawing before going over the blending system a few more times.

Stage 3: Mixing the foundation we then, mixed this in with an oil paint diluting, which made a streamlined under drawing.
Stage 4: We decided to use pastels in varying etchings in moderate layers to add surface to your drawing as required.

Stage 5: Scratch beguiling nuances, In the last season of the drawing, we used a show up at edge to fix nuances like branches, stays aware of and the skyline between the trees.

USE OIL PASTELS TO MAKE STRIKING CRAFTSMANSHIP

You can make very close drawings with a lot of surface and shocking tones using oil pastels. They are extremely easy to use and can be used to snap a photograph in an outstandingly short degree of time. Oil pastels are by and large challenging to work with, but when you gain proficiency with a couple of fundamental methodology, they're not excessively hard to try and consider using. Oil pastels offer a vital set that would be useful whether you are a refined skilled worker just start or a capable expert who necessities to add to their grouping. They're versatile, bendable and open in a colossal hotshot of striking shades.

FOSTER YOUR VIEWPOINTS WITH DELICATE PASTELS

Despite how they are on an extraordinarily fundamental level explicit from oil pastels, delicate pastels are right now ready for making remarkable drawings. They have a fine consistency like chalk, which makes them ideal for blending.

THE END

www.ingramcontent.com/pod-product-compliance
Lightning Source LLC
Chambersburg PA
CBHW071002290526
45795CB00005B/1757